# PASSPORT STAMPS

Maria Eloise Baza

Copyright © 2020 Maria Eloise Baza

All rights reserved

The characters and events portrayed in this book are fictitious. Any similarity to real persons, living or dead, is coincidental and not intended by the author.

No part of this book may be reproduced, or stored in a retrieval system, or transmitted in any form or by any means, electronic, mechanical, photocopying, recording, or otherwise, without express written permission of the publisher.

ISBN: 9798644843886

Cover design by: Asalya Djuraeva

Library of Congress Control Number: 2018675309
Printed in the United States of America

*To the places
that I've been to and lived,
loving you was easy*

# INTRODUCTION

It's beautiful to look out the window and gaze at the clouds as the plane passed over the snowy mist. It'll only be thirteen more hours until the plane lands in London, England. I wished it wouldn't take so long to see you on the other side. I wished for us to drive down Londontown together. It'll be like the first time. But that will have to wait, I'm still on my way back to you.

I started flicking through the films they have. Nothing was of my interest but I had to pick something just to keep my mind off the loneliness without you. I saw Passport to Paris, Sleepless in Seattle, What Happened In Vegas, and Letters to Juliet. Honey, I want to see the world with you if you'd only take me there.

Just landed at Heathrow Airport, I got past immigration and the long dreary line towards the gates. When I got out, I hesitated. I saw you standing there. You won't believe me when I say that you were the only thing I saw... You.

You and your ocean blues. You and your starlit smile under fluorescent lights that never do you justice. Baby, let's go!

Our story started like this:

Small town girl meets a man with a boyish charm and an earnest reputation to uphold. A coffee cup in his hand and a King

Charles Spaniel in the other. It had her attention as he attempted to take a call. She could tell that he was having a little trouble but he was too much of a man to ask for her help.

He was a little frustrated, stressed out. He yelled at her. She called him ill-tempered. Worse of all, ruthless. For she did not utter a single word that was out of offense. He just took it like it was.

Love can be ever so blinding at times when you don't see the things screaming at you from day one, darling. Love can be limitless. We give love for the sake of giving love even when they don't deserve it. Love can be a stamp on your passport on your way to spend the summer abroad and to take the time off for yourself. Love can be something that you've seen on the street while walking your dog.

If you don't believe me, just travel the world and watch the people talk about love like it's a film or a play. It's a beautiful sight to see.

Love,
Maria
xo

## *To All The Boys*

To all the boys that I've ever met, here's what I think of you. You are only around when my reputation's gone south. You see... People only misunderstand what I do. I go into something with no intentions.

Funny isn't it. It's funny how I just woke up one morning and said, "let's give all these boys a heart attack."

I'm not stupid. I know that whispers are the tabloids of college. You live in a world that I once loved.

Mr Fireplace, I used to... You thought that I liked you but I didn't. That's troubling.

Trouble? Now, that we're on the topic of trouble...

To the illogical rocket, you never seem to seek answers. You only go by your stupid logic. You misunderstood me, my friend. Friend? Hell. You could've been my best friend. Cause, you know, I saw you as a sibling. And you argue with your siblings, intensely. I've been there before. Funny how history repeats itself.

To all the boys that I've ever met, here's to my delicate reputation.

## *Rip Off The Page*

page by page, darling
rip it off like a bandage
turn the Page, one or two
the wheels kept turning

she'd hope to burn her past
she'd hope to keep it hidden
she'D hope that no one noticed,
no one at all

crazy family members
rip off the page!
people think we're toXic
rip off the page!

prideful people screaming,
just shrug your shoulders, girl
When you get a papercut,
And bleed, rip off the page!

## *Three Christmases*

She's a two month old flower,
Just waiting to fully blossom
She heard their loud voices,
Echoing around the room

Snow-colored plastic tree on a table
Decorated in shiny gold tinsel and lights
Frank Sinatra, Fred Astaire
Liven-ing it up on the stereo

She's a seven year old flower,
Standing on a cold Welsh street
She saw snow covering the ground
For the very, very first time

Tall plastic Christmas evergreens
Decorated in ruby glass baubles
People pileing on like rugbymen
Smile on her face, nothing to fear

She's twenty-four now as a flower
With a few tricks up her sleeves,
Dreaming of a new white Christmas
And the cold air blew towards her

Cutting it down on a Christmas Tree Farm
In her brown coat drinking hot cider
Standing by a small fireplace, quiet
Still the music roared in her ears

## *Dandelion Wishes*

Used to pick up white dandelions
Off the grass and blow them away
Pretty much the highlight of my day

Remembered that Welsh breeze,
Blowing through my raven hair
That feels like home sweet home

A twelve year old, Lent Lily
Making welsh cakes
With the ladies of the backroom

Singing praises in a choir
Dressed in white cloaks
And Father Thomas' jokes

Daydreamed for a better
Tomorrow than my yesterdays
When worse comes to worse

Used to wish on dandelions
All summer long in my youth
It was my eleven, eleven

## *Maria*

Maria lived a fairytale life
And she was happy.

She'd light candles on
her Granddaughters' birthdays:

One in flooding August,
Another in sunny December.

Maria is an angel with gold wings
And her light still shines in two.

## *Solitaire*

You're picking up the broken pieces
like you have everything to lose.
You don't have to, darling.

People are calling you names.
People judge you because you know
some things they don't know.

You get called delusional
But honey, believe in your own crazy
As I've done in the past.

You'll hear the radio singing
"we're tied together with a smile",
just believe it, darling.

## *Him*

He is enchanting like the moonlight
He lets me shine brighter than the stars
He is dangerous like no one I've been with
It's like a shot in the dark without him
He gives this blind love a brand new page
I'm his darling balancing on a tightrope

## *By The Fire*

By the fire,
November arises.
No fumes in sight
But flames take flight.

To him, it was nothing.
To her, it was ev'rything

Each beat, each ticking
Of the clock...
She felt safely secured!

## *American Boy*

American Boy,
My name in his lips
To curse, to burn.
I was only nothing.

American Boy,
Full of pride
But nothing else
In his cold heart.

Oh, how dumb
I was? I fell for
An American Boy
With a mind like his.

## *Landline*

The phone rang and rang
Her mind was empty
Her head spun around
In multiple, multiple circles

Caller I.D.: Fire Hazard
He wanted to know
She didn't breathe a word
And deleted his number

Her landline was shut
For days, for years
He wrote her a letter
She didn't want to know

## *He Said*

He threw me into a riot
That left me badly bruised.
He burnt me into a fire
That got me screaming.

He went around saying
That I was delusional
When I've created
A universe in my head.

He said that I was crazy
But honey, I'm only me.
He said that I was useless
But what's the use of him.

He went around,
Waving the rainbow flag.
It's no use in pride
When it's all, you know.

He's dressed in black
When I've made it clear
That I'm here for me
And not for him.

Whatever he said,
It doesn't even matter.
He was only a name
To cross off in red ink.

## St. James Park

You acted so cold to protect a love
that was merely a circus performance.
A spectacle you were stuck in
for three cruel months.

And now, you're on your knees
wanting me to have you.

Oh, hell no!

You chose the circus life
over the private love.
It'll be a relative disaster
for the both of us.

Remember St. James Park?
That was when you knew
the truth about her
But you didn't believe
my kind heart.

## *Stupid Boy*

You're the tin man
without a beating heart.
I am Dorothy Gale standing alone
in the pouring rain until the sun shines
through a cloudy day.

You're the monster under my bed
that I feared as a child.
I longed to know you,
to know the real you as I sit here wondering
what made you colder than before.

You said that you knew better than me.
I thought that you knew better than me.

I wish you weren't
the stupid boy
that you are
TODAY!

That's NOT the boy
I once knew.

## *Empty*

Thought that we'd be light years away
From a world full of angels and demons,
Knowing what was used to be of us.
Came here for freedom, isn't that enough?

Darling, how I spent my days thinking
America's full of centerfolded dreams?
When so many people made me believe,
America is full of empty hearts and pride.

## Castles Crumbling

There's a crown sat on the throne of revenge,
but people still whisper in the hall,
"she's a bad, bad girl, a rebel"
"she's a fake, a phony"
"she's dishonest, she betrays."
"you just can't trust a girl like that."
And that was when she fell apart
without a king to rescue her.

## The Timeless Firefly

She saw the plainness of his words
Like a firefly under the moonlight.
It was timeless just like a disco ball.
She'd believe to be truer than true.
Jane and Emily aged her mind
With tales, she'd only dreamed and
The choir sung a thousand songs
But none were about the devil's words.

## *Lavenders*

Lavenders are the roses of the French.
It can be scattered like starlight.
Though mystical and beautiful,
It can't be a wish for a million dreamers.

## Beautiful Night

You were an English boy
In the Scottish breeze
And it feels like home.
When fireworks blossomed
On the purple, blue sky,
It's such a beautiful night
With you!

## *Honeymooners*

We were dancin' 'round
the living room floor
While the neighbours
pound the door

To the radio
and our favourite song,
I'm in your arms
where I truly belong

## *Didn't You Know That?*

Crimson lips, Vixenous waves
A bad girl in denim jeans
Called out for the way, she acts
Known for the way, she moves

She doesn't hear the end of it
Through the whispers, it's all negative

If it were you, you'd take a stand
She's sitting there taking it all in
She's heard it all before
Boy, didn't you know that?

Pretty in pink, Thinks with the music
Say she has a rebellious streak,
Has nothing going on for her-self,
But always something mindless to do

She doesn't hear the end of it
Through the whispers, it's all negative

If it were you, you'd take a stand
She's sitting there taking it all in
She's heard it all before
Boy, didn't you know that?

You scream for your own sanity
She screams cause she has to

## *Uneasy*

When he calls out a name,
He says it in a different tune.
She haven't heard it before.
It was a different symphony
Than what they played in '95.
But whatever she said in '08,
It seemed like an uneasy setback.

*Red*

Red is the roses
you gave to me
on the fourteenth.

But those love songs
they played on the radio
always made me cry
like how you
changed your mind
on the fifteenth.

Red.
It burns like
hell fire…

If I'm not enough,
I'll just let these
roses fade
away…

I guess, no one told me
who you really are
when all is…
    BLIND!

## Dirty Game

I thought of everything about you.
When it came to me breaking apart,
You had my best interest at heart.
I always saw the best view in you.

You're spinning me around and around
To the beat of your own drums,
Making my burst out laughing
And your dirty jokes means everything.

You had on those dirty blue jeans.
The ones painted your bedroom walls with
In the shade of gray, you liked so much.
I'm leaning against the wall... Smiling.

You kissed me quick, once or twice.
Our clothes scattered on the floor.
I'm in nothing but the darkest lace.
Felt my heart beat, rapidly and sweetly.

We played a dirty game for hours.
I've never expected that from you.
Took a few pictures under the covers,
And locked in a warm embrace.

Loved how you made me feel like
I'm the only girl in the world.
Everything I knew passes into thin air
When I'm with you, my darling.

## *Salem Witch*

Embers falling to the ground
Like snow on Christmas day
Burning out in the rain
She surpasses all judgement

People are united against her
With their pitch forks
And their proofs

She burnt like a piece of clay
And dusted herself on the floor
She was wrong by Salem
They found her a criminal

## Joan of Arc

Had nothing left but the rags on her back
Kept her head up high like Joan of Arc
No family left alive to defend her
But the demons from her childhood
Had burnt her ALIVE!

The heathens and their grievings
Angel Gabriel and his spear,
Vanished from sight
Her screams, deathening
The witch was no more…

## *Goodbye Butterfly*

Before he calls me up...
Before he makes up lies...
Before he wants to ask me...
I just want him to know
Darling, I can see through him
I see through his "pain"
And that's not okay

He pretended to suffer on a cross
Because I was actually right
He cried like a baby in its crib
Because he wants to be always right
Dumb! Dumb Butterfly!
It was all nonsense to me
I just wanted it to be over

He burnt the letters I sent to him
I burnt his paintings in a bonfire
He turned everything into ashes
I crashed his pride into a mud
It was a warzone like never before
He played the victim card
Goodbye! Goodbye Butterfly!

## *Twelve*

There was, this saying
That all good things
Must come to an end,
And things starts to bend.
There are walls built,
To stand the hurricanes.

At twelve,
Bridges are crossed
Mountains are climbed
But often play pretend
As we go 'bout the day
Our minds tend to evolve.

Everyone has their monsters
That they hide from.
Everyone has their monsters
That they're shutting out
From the people's eyes,
And from their ears.

No one in their minds
Wants all of the good
To come, a full stop!
Adjust, getting to know
Someone you just met.
Welcome to hell!

## *Merci Ensuite*

This girl picked up a pen
And I wrote about you.

I wouldn't be doing this
if you didn't burn me
like a Salem Witch.

Darling, I'm not delusional
Nor am I the crazy one.
I'm just doing my thing
and I'm doing it right.

## *Unity*

We are all one in a million.
All with different voices.
All with a mindful journey.

We grow up in different ways.
We are all human.
We make mistakes.
We cry. We hurt.

Most importantly,
We all have a story to tell.

## Our White Christmas

Remember when little girls
Dance around in golden dresses
On the road, under the moonlight
Singing carols on a September morning
It was a Christmas in the province

You have cousins from another world
That you haven't spoken to in a while
Seen pictures of their life, all in white
Frozen trees, rain comes in glistening
It was their Christmas in the city

Remember those adolescent boys
On an Easter afternoon,
Walking down the road
Fun is what's on their minds
Oh, those were the days

Dreamt of a snowy white haven
And the golden aftermath
Girls in pastry-shaped dresses
And broken lipstick on the floor
That could be any day now

Flash forward to that November
In the cold Korean street
Lighting up the sky by candlelight
Walking through the province
Like we knew our way around

Darling, love will be our White Christmas
That we've been dreaming of, as kids

Oh, my darling, take me all the way back
Take me back to that November morning
That will forever be embedded in my heart

## *Ours*

Days goes by like blue embers
We fought a 17 year battle,
just to find it.

We all see all the
different colours
of the rainbow.

Hope is the loudest thing to
ever come between us.

## The Battle of Egos

Everyone's cutting out the innocent
Burnt things in their path,
They can't handle

Worried by everything and by nothing
They made her believe, she was at fault
They saw how she acts,
How she played the field,
Making everything vanish like that

When she fought a long war,
Lived in the trenches,
Suffered from disease,
At what cost?

It doesn't make sense
Her world spun in circles
When they fought against her,
Not with her

She didn't fight on the battlefield
That took twenty months to mend
And another to regain the throne,
She lost along the way.

## The Queen's Lament

He is King of the Ancien Régime
He had the heart of gold
Queen of the Golden Pearls
She wanted nothing more
Met on the Battle of the Coast

His shattering ocean blues
Her deep chestnut views
The beating of the drums
A thousand swords in the air
Prum! Tum! Tum! Prum! Tum! Tum!

"Prepare for the battle, Britannia,"
She said, "blood will spill!"
Horses galloped to one another
For hours, and hours on end
Her crown fell off her horse

Taken captive by the King,
The King of Britannia
It was an alliance by marriage
Or none at all, the axe, death
Her blood spilled at his pleasure

They collided like the clashing of swords
She was gazing on his beating heart
His arms locking her into an embrace,
Pushing her down on to her knees
His dagger dangled in front of her

Took it from him as she begged to him
That made him grin from ear to ear

She wanted no alliance but freedom
The freedom of Tagalonians, her people.
Hers can be ceased into his possessions

His dagger cut into her
And felt her body gave in
As he heard the voices of his men,
Beating into the femininity of her realm
It was beautiful sound to hear

He did the crime, she paid for it
He knelt down in sight, she collapsed
He grabbed her, she was drowsy
He laid her down on a marshmallow haven
Again he caged her holding on so tightly

The sound of laughter lingered inside
As night turned into new day
Her dress was like the snow
Contrasting the darkness of her hair
The band played, the people stood

This was what she agreed to
Gracefully placing her hand on his,
The Priest spoke the words, she'd dread
She must now play the part of the wife
To a man who she hated all her life

## It's Truly Complicated!

Trapped in a love affair
That went nowhere
She felt like a ghost
In her own marriage

Betrayed by her husband,
And her friend
And damaged her corset,
And her satin dress

Broke her crown and left his side
She wrote it down, all of it
From his lonely words,
To her tears of desperation

Every lost words ended up
On the cutting room floor
The snippets of negatives
Never made the final cut

People thought her crazy,
Never knew why they did
She bled from cuts
And accused of rebellion

## *Be Alright*

Rain is the pain inside of me
I caught myself falling from my flight
Then you came in and swept me away
I should've known the way you danced,
The way you waltz down the road

You made me feel like I'm flying,
Like I'm soaring with no wings
You're the angle I'm looking for
Please, be right by my side
And I'll be alright

I hope to see you again
You know it's not the same
Without our time alone
It's not like the last time
We cruised through the sea

You made me feel like flying
Like we're soaring through the clouds
You were the angel I've dreamed of
Just be right by my side
And I'll be alright

This December,
I hope that you find
Who you're looking for
I hope you make her feel like flying
Like she's soaring with no wings
Cause I'm not the angel you're looking for

You know, I knew about it

MARIA BAZA

That she'll be right by your side
That it wouldn't be me

## *Believe It Or Not*

No one's freaky enough
To break it down like you.
It's not insanity…
It's just how you feel it

Believe it or not,
You're dancing on a graveyard
You can go flying if you want
Believe it or not,
We were a tragedy to begin with
We couldn't last forever

Loving you was a hardship
You drive me down sometimes
And it taunts my mind

## The First Date

She's his Bonnie Parker
Wanting that thrill ride.
He's her Shakespeare
Acting out a fairytale.

## NYC

They say New York City
is the city of dreams,
but look at me in the eye
and tell me I'm the dream.

## *Betrayal*

I signed my name
on the dotted line
and claimed by fame.
Regardless of all the pain,
I will always be his
And his alone, my dear.

## *Wasted*

All the wasted times
For this wasted love
That I spent on you.
It ain't the best view.

## *Mine*

It's harder to see
your not Mine
When all my world
is crumbling like I'm
Barefoot on
Brown glass.

## *Rumours*

I guess, all the rumours are true
He makes me see the best view
And he makes it last

## *Gabriela*

What would Gabriela Silang do?
Would she fight for peace
and prosperity? Would she adapt
into a world of war? No,
she would fight for truth,
justice, and the independence
of her nation.

## *Gilda*

The Gilda in me
wouldn't care
about what people
thinks of her interior.

The Gilda in me
wouldn't care
if people saw her
at her worse
and not at her best.

The Gilda in me
would love herself
despite having
a broken heart.

## *Powerhouse*

Taylor wrote you
into her music.
I wrote you
into my poetry.
There's no escaping
the women who built
you into a powerhouse name.

## *Found It*

Thought you were alone
Seeing your friends find it
(They finally found it)

Childhood crushes and friends
Y'know, I'm with you
where the Scottish wind blows
And it blows!!!

## *Tuesday's Deals*

There's this small town
Only a few hundred people
live there and knew its name

It's always crowded
on a Tuesday
filled with people
trying to get the best deals

People calls it
a mess of a town
But it's home to me

## *Dear You*

Dear you,
You are enough.

Dear you,
You are brave
and you are stronger
than you think.

Dear you,
I love you.

## Loved You

If I loved you again,
I wouldn't mind the stereo on blast
while we're jamming out to Gloria
in the car on our way to Astoria, OR

## *Crimson*

In your wildest dreams,
You see me with a crimson smile
Looking at you like a devil in a dress

## *Polariod*

I can't love you again
but when I do, if I do
I'll take a polaroid of us

## *Welcome Distraction*

I know —
— about her.
She's the one
You've loved
before I came
along so I put
pen to paper
and wrote
about you
in one of my
poetry, babe.

I've let her music
inspire me but I can't
seem to get you
out of my mind.

You and your
blue greens.

And that jaded
look you had
like those love
doves that got
me burnt.

But when
it comes down
to you,
you are a
"Welcome
Distraction"

## *I Don't Know Why*

As I'm writing to you,
I don't know why...

I don't know why
I love you
But I do...
I do love you with all my heart

## *What Love Was*

I didn't know what love was
until you came along
playing our song
on your guitar

Singing songs
that we've heard
on the radio

I heard you
whisper I love you
in the dark
that was when
I felt what love was

## Close To You

Close to you like the sound
of the sambas they play
And to the sound
of my beating heart

His ocean blues
takes me places
I've never been to

## Hot Water

He's trailing on hot water
when I kiss his lips.
He's trailing on hot water
when I catch him
in the act of his lies.
God, may I love the devil?
As he loved me?

## *Purity*

How can I find a love so pure?
They deny all desperations
But it's you who I see as home.
It's you who captured my beating heart.

## Baby Blues

He's six foot tall
and his beautiful baby blues
staring right back at me

I never found him again
But I'd never found anyone new

He's all I've got
until we've come
together again,
darling

Throughout the city's lights
I'll love you through and through

## *Drowning*

You caught me screaming freedom
When I'm already out of the ocean,
Out of the blue...
But we're stuck, back in the trenches
And I'm drowning, drowning, drowning
And caught in a thunder storm, babe
You better just catch me in your arms

## Heartbreak Road

Fireworks in the sky
I see your English eyes
As we drive down the busy street.

Get us outta here,
I wanna fly!

Let's get lost until next season
As people blows their time.

I came here from
Vancouver, British Columbia
one way just to see you.

## Golden Girl

Misunderstood
How can you know?
No questions asked.
Just two crazy minds.

And when you are invincible,
You think you're invincible
While I'm invisible to you.
To a crowd of thousands,
I disappear into thin air.
I wanted what you left
in this world.
You were enough for me.

I'm under the sun
with peppermint sunglasses
I felt the cold air
as pink cotton candy clouds
pass on by.

You make those grey clouds
disappear into the blues of your guitar.
And those dark long nights can't
keep your love away from me.

Darling, I'm your Golden Girl
with the golden heart.

Every song reminds me of you,
I wouldn't stop thinking of you.
The universe tells me,
"Come on!

It won't be anyone else but him.
It's destiny!"

## *Family*

Family is the Careless Whisper.
You'll see in the dark.
They'll never hate.
They'll always love.

## *True Love*

True Love has nothing
to do with fairytales.
It hasn't been magical.

True Love is rare.
It's the fight
that will have
at 3 am.
It'll keep us
up all night
until we make it up
alright.

True Love is like a Wedding Vow.
It's passion and commitment.
It's the final white dress
that I'll get to wear.
And that's when I'll know
that your love is true.

## *Bonnie & Clyde*

We ran the world
like Bonnie & Clyde
with gunshots
across the ivory sky
and a story that's worth
a hundred to one

## *Fifth Avenue*

I'm skipping stones
on Fifth Avenue
as we're dancing
on the sidewalk
with your guitar
singing the songs
I wrote about us.

I knew that somehow
you were too extreme
but I loved the way
you loved me.

I'm skipping rocks
on Fifth Avenue.
Heartbeats skipping
on the sidewalk
like a million names
falling slowly off the top
but I loved the way
I loved you.

## *Love Is*

Love is like the smell of roses in the dark
And not like a lost glove
When it comes to seeing you
for the first time

Love is like a spectrum of colours
Turning into something beautiful.

Love ain't something
that happens over night.
It's limitless!

## *Her Sweet Escape*

The busy streets
And the pink laces
scattered on the floor
And her sweet escape

## *Rainbow*

Flowers blooming in the sun's rays
As she drives towards the stars
And all the colours of the rainbow
Began to fade into nothing.

## *Between Us*

How can I let this
feeling come between us?
It's like a spiraling sorrow
to my heart.

## *Peg Entwistle*

I feel like Peg Entwistle
climbing to the top
of the Hollywood sign.

A mess of a London girl
with nothing, just nothing
to look forward to.

I feel like the world
came crashing down on me
as I cry my heart out.

A mess of a Manila girl
with only her poetry
to get her by the ropes.

## *Wild Ride*

This is who I'm going to be
Leader of the free world
Running in the name of freedom
Running a wild, wild ride

## *Right Words*

I don't know
how to tell him this
But the right words
seems to slip right thru

## Lucky Stars

You fit my poems
like a lost glove
in December.
And I thank my lucky stars
love don't end
in embers.

## *Phoenix*

Draw your sword
Take the stand
Gather your army
And see if I budge
or give my crown up.

I see through your disruption,
your violent ideals.

The phoenix raises
off the ashes.

## *Bonneville*

In Bonneville,
he's running wild with the boys.
I'm in the corner again,
rolling my eyes like
I don't give a damn
or I couldn't careless.

In Bonneville,
where the sunshines
when I'm with you
and little girls skipping rocks
in the pond.

In Bonneville,
where home is
what we make of it.
In Bonneville,
where I loved you so.

## *Red Eye*

I caught the
Red Eye
just to
see you again

I never
thought
of a
love so
pure
when it
comes to the love
in your heart.

But I wanted
to fly to you
And see a great
view…

*Battle*

Armour fields
Disruption ways
Blood on the floor
I've had enough
Screaming into a wild flame
Poison saved me

## *Saint*

We all play the victim
But never the saint
We all have sacrifices
But never in the same season
We don't see who we are until all is lost

## *Scotland Yard*

I've had you all
figured out like
I'm Sherlock Holmes
in Scotland Yard
But I can't seem
to put it all
together again...

## Cherry Tree

Falling softly,
Falling slowly
like a cherry
trees in May.

Birds chirping in the sunny skies
But when the truth comes out,
It'll only hurt her!

## The Perfect Man

I fell for a villain
that never knew me.
But boy,
was he perfect
in every way.

## *Marilyn Monroe*

I can be selfish
I can be fearsome
I can be seen alone
Is this how Marilyn Monroe felt?

Is this how she must've felt?
I can be seen dancing around
Trying to make mends
To what is right
Rather than what is wrong

## *Enchanted*

My darling,
I blamed you for nothing
And you blamed me too
But on that night
I was enchanted
to meet you.

I knew that you'd drown
in your own sick
and twisted arena
But honey,
I was enchanted
to see you again.

## *Erase You*

I'll erase you from my memory
I'll erase you from my brain
But no one came close
To loving me but you
And that's the best view
His eyes of blue so pure

*Fool*

You treated me like a fool
I was a circus clown
in your perfect show

But I didn't want
to be that girl anymore

I wanted to be the girl
whose dreamed to be beside you.

## *Violinist*

You put me higher
than you do with her
But still, you love her
like you've always done

And if I stayed,
you'll be the violinist
that played with my heart

We're better off
six feet apart,
darling

*Pandemic*

We rise from the ashes
Like a phoenix
But we deliver
Like a pandemic

## *Fiddle*

You play your cards
like you've play your fiddle
And I'm always in the middle
of nothing, and everything

You're pulling me apart
like it was a lifeline
I can not hold on to
whereas we can be something

You play the minor chords
as I heard the final vow
Alas, your sweet melody
plays through my veins

## *Virtue*

Delicacy is a virtue
It is not power
It is not the used-to-be's
It is the moment you saw me
Standing there, smiling
Like a careful girl
Standing in the rainstorm

Alcohol plays the minor role
While the back of your hand
played a major role
in breaking me apart
Love is a virtue
That you overtook
I hated you for that

## *I Don't Know*

I don't know
what to do
without you

I don't know
what to do
with you

I don't know
what to do
anymore...

## *Heathens*

Missing you is...
The dark blue skies
The golden red sun rise

But loving you
is like an endless chord
that the heathens may play

Fighting you is...
like those pesky cats
and those ratchet dogs

But loving you
is like an endless winter
and our footsteps on
the snowy white ground

## *How I Roll*

I'll roll with the hipsters
and the artists.

You'll see me with
the painters and
the actors.

But you'll never see me
with the liars and
the dirty cheats
of the world.

## *Used*

I used to be
your Anne Hathway,
your Juliet Capulet,
your everything.

But I wasn't the girl
in your history.
The one you loved before.

## *Lost*

When I was drowning
and lost at sea,
I felt the smokey atmosphere
burn through the sky
I knew that I couldn't breathe
any longer

I thought that flying
would forget you
but flying only failed
to pay the price of fame

## *Love Is Louder*

Love is louder
than any of those
high school remarks.

Love is louder
than what others
may think of you.

Love is louder
than perfection.

*Loki*

Hell is empty
There's a hundred
chimes of the bell
and saw nothing
But the devils
gathering around him

He isn't all bad
But my darling,
He can benefit from
the love of a home
Like the first time
you took my heart

## *Sirens*

Hear the sirens call my name
It will defy those of belittles
Love comes to those who believes
in taking chances, and risks

But still,
I hear myself
cry at night

I'm calling out a name
that was yours
and all the pain that came with it

Let me hear it again
Let me hear the sirens
call my name to
pardoned by my goodbyes

## *Hey American Boy*

Hey American Boy,
If you don't want me then
Why am I the last name
On your lips?

Hey American Boy,
If I wasn't prepared then
Why did people applaud
For me, darling?

Hey American Boy,
If you want space then
Why do you have
Another in your arms?

## *Fly Away*

I'll fly to you
I'll fly away
I'll fly to find
myself again

Darling,
I'll fly away
to spread
my wings

I'll fly away
until you want me again

I'll fly away
until you remember
who was there to love you

## *Taylor Swift*

If I'm missing you, should I write you
in my poetry like Taylor Swift?
Knowing all your favourite songs,
Could you be the one to rescue me?
Could you be the one to help me fly?

If I'm needing you,
Should I think of you
The way that I do?
Knowing that you'll disappear like a ghost
Through these velveteen skies.

But you're not here,
Nowhere to be found.
But these endless days,
Come forth like clockworks.

## *She'd Be The Reason*

She'd be the reason
why you die a little

She'd be the reason
why you don't truly see you

She'd be the reason
why we don't see eye to eye

She'd be the reason
why I'm not with you

## *Time*

How would time fly by
if I weren't with you?
What will time say?
How I've lost and gained?

But in all honesty, you couldn't stop.
You couldn't stop thinking of you
And you alone.

Yet you are the Hercules
to this Megara.

You're like a knife
cutting through me
when you speak.

I wished for you
to know me by heart
but you couldn't love me.

## I Remember

I remember the embers
that flew onto my hair.
I remember the flightless birds
from that August night.
I remember you and I
skipping along the pavement
overlooking the trees.
But the memory of you
flickers like candlelight.

## *Untitled Traces*

We light the skies
like fireworks on the 4th of July.
I see you like no one else,
but you run the world
like someone's watching.

Darling, if I were you,
I wouldn't be dancing
like that, Trace.
I would be soaring through
these pastel skies.

## *Honey Baby*

We light the skies
like fireworks on the 4th of July.
I see you like no one else,
but you run the world
like someone's watching.

Darling, if I were you,
I wouldn't be dancing
like that, Trace.
I would be soaring through
these pastel skies.

## *Stay*

When I first met Trace,
I braced myself for
the longest time.

I held my head
up high to
last a goodbye.

I hated the
sound of my
own voice
asking him
to stay,
but I did anyway.

## *Knowing*

Light pink skies.
Diamonds that flies.
Love that flatters.
Morning dues.
You're that one thing
that made me brand new.

You gave me hope
as I run away from you.
I see a brighter view
than ever before.
You saw right through the lies
that they told me.

You were once a friend
that burned my daisies.
I saw right through your mistakes
like the day that you made me one.
Darling, you don't know me all too well.
You don't know me at all.

## *Home*

If home is where the heart is,
then why am I counting down
the days until I see you again?
As I walk down memory lane,
there's no other end
but you and I, all over again.
Now that I'm on my own,
are you still wanting me right
by your side again?

## *Another Love*

Love makes us all breathless.
It lingers through our skins.
One step or another more.

You took me dancing that night
under the moonlight sky.
Held me closer to your chest.

Yet, I'm fooled once again
by your words, and yours alone.
Love is what you make of it
and I'm breathless, once more.

## *Boleyn*

Bewithered by the storm.
Room filled with ball gowns
And corsets scattered on the floor
While music filled the room.

I see you standing there
As bare as can be
Joyful as a man could become.
You are the soul of the sun.

You took me by surprise.
Darling, I never saw it coming.
You standing there to rescue me
Hoping that I'd play the part of wife.

Nevertheless, you took an oath
my dear before we wed
that I could still see your shining face
Blossom through the clouds.

## The Axe

Many thing blows with the winds:
The trees that haunted me,
The clouds that gazed down from the skies.

You seemed like a man
worth longing for
but you're not that man.

You played me like a fool
once the music played
and that I did not see.

## *The Truth About Eve*

She'd bewitched so many
and so many that came to her.
She has him bewitched by
a song through the records.
That's the truth about Eve.

She would cradle him
like endless fires through the storm
that carried through the snow.
She's insatiable.
That's the truth about Eve.

Her song comes and goes
like clockworks through time.
She'd witness the crows
singing at twilight.
That's the truth about Eve.

She had bewitched him too.
Nothing to fight for but her own wit
and her own rainstorm.
She is bewitching by sight.
That's the truth about Eve.

## *Before the Storm*

Before the storm passes on,
I'd die a thousand times.

Before you play hard to get,
I'd worship a God above.

Before you carry me off,
I'd stand back,
watch a Queen conquer.

## *The Essence of Me*

I had my time away from him.
It was something I needed,
Something that I wanted.
I've been played like strings.

My heart of gold is pure.
My hair so luxurious.
My love unlike any other.
I've been played by my time.

Cut down from the tree of wisdom.
I'm not sorry for the words I've said.
I'm only sorry for the words I never said.
I am but a figure of the sun and the moon.

Darling, that's the essence of me.
Never to become cut from the stars.

## *Wild Life*

Say you'll remember the girl
standing there in her best dress
with nothing to lose
but herself in the view.

And she'll overcome her fears
just to see you again, my dear.
Cause darling, we are one,
We are one in all its glory.

My friend to be clearer.
I was once in love
with the aspects of beauty.
I was once yours to toy with.

She'll shed some light on her feelings
Just like she shed all the toxicity,
you came with, my sweet.
But always remember me
and that dress from long ago.

## *What If*

What if our stars would align?
What if our paths would collide?

What if I remembered why I loved you?
What if I remembered why I got up and left?

What if you were always there for me?
What if...
What if...

We'll always be a what if.
Never an always will be.

## *Sparks*

When sparks fly,
I see myself shine through.

When romance is gone,
I can be the witch
to see all things through.

When days turn into night,
I can't turn myself in.

## *Darling*

Darling, you're my daydream
from another time, another life.
I seem to forget what it's like
to dance in ball gowns
and corsets so tight.

Darling, I written so many letters
and signed them with your last name.
In my blood, I've loved, I've bled
knowing that we've got no end.

Darling, I wasn't ready to see it,
to see a life flash before my eyes.

## *Perfect*

Perfect have I loved
All is gone with a dance
And in the darkness, bewithered
Oh, how perfect we could be

Perfect have I played
All is weathered by the rain
And all of the pain will go away
How much perfect could we be

Oh, should I tell
the world of us?
Or should I listen to
the bewitching sound
of silence?

## *Lucifer*

To him,
I'm Lucifer hailing from the south.
I am but a lady all dressed in satin.

To him,
I'm a villainess with nothing to lose.
I am the lady from his worse of fears.

To him,
I'm nothing but a nightmare in a dress.

To me,
I can do most anything
my heart's desires.

## *Paint Me*

All these bitches,
They paint me red.
All these rebels,
They have been shaken.

In my bed, I have read
that all these monsters
end with nothing but
the blood that took my hand.

In the end, I'm painted
As the villainess
Who's up to no good.

## *Idle Senses*

Help me hold on to what used to be
Or what might have been...
My heart renders me speechless.
My idle senses tortures me through.

I could listen to the radio
But the radio seems
to remind me of you.

I could walk a mile
But each step reminds me of you.

I wanted so much for all
the memory of you
To fade away...

I'm not one to reminisce about the past
But I'm sick of that same old filth
that you fed me once upon a time.
It's never changing but I believed them.

Oh, how you turned me into the fool.
When I was young and naïve at 16.

## *Serendipity*

Things aren't too different
Things often finds a way
to measure up into something
Not just the idea of something

There's no something
without the love of a friend,
the love of someone
so sincere

I think it's the way
We measure up to people
that defines us as people

We have to believe
in who we used to be
to figure out
what we truly believe in

Trust in what is kind,
what is the lawful truth
that is serendipity

## *Homesick*

If I'm lost,
will you find me?

If I'm alone,
will you keep me company?

If I'm homesick,
will you bring me back home again?

Sometimes I feel lost
Sometimes I feel alone

Sometimes I feel like Marilyn Monroe
But I'm never always homesick

## Scars

darling, let
the scars go
there will
always be
another one
that will
make your
stars shine

## *Lifetime*

Love is splendor
It's worth the wait
It'd worth every waking
hour of the day
It only happens
once in a lifetime
I'd wait for you

## *American Story*

Abigail wrote
to John
a letter

She said that
she'll forever be his
for all time

She added
"remember the ladies"
and that he did
for America
to shine bright

John didn't keep
his promise
but it was
only a matter
of time
for things
to begin
to change

He wanted the fame
and the fortune
to last a lifetime
but only her love lasted

They were the kind
of love that never withered
but they were only human

MARIA BAZA

They fought like cats and dogs
In privacy, they're the standard
American story told
by many generations

Abigail had love
in hopeless times
in warlike days
in redemption
for a new world

John died
on the 4th of July
Abigail followed
soon thereafter
But they had
a love that
was so pure.

## *History*

You'd wish that
I'd come running, running
But that's unlike me
You tore our little girl
apart like she was only dust
like she was crying out

To tell you the truth,
She's doing well
She wrote this
to you, hoping you'd stay
but you didn't
She only blamed herself
but I know,
she'll make history somehow.

# COME DECEMBER

*A Short Story*

# HIDDEN AGENDAS

Anyone and everyone will tell you that High School is the most funnest four years that you'll have in one town. That wasn't the same feeling that had when I first walked through the doors of my freshman year.

Everyone were like hounds, like aggressive British bulldogs, like a lost puppy gathering into the L-shaped hallway. I was the lost puppy. I didn't seem to fit in with everybody else.

It was bad. It was worse than bad.

Driven with a puff of invisible smoke over my head, I walked down the L-shaped hallway. That hallway was packed with hundreds of students barging through the crowd as they attempt to make their way towards their classes in under five minutes. It felt like rush hour in New York City on a not-so busy day.

My denim jacket scraped by people passing by pass me. I held my head up high as I entered my home room. I was greeted by the star of David pinned in between two window pane. I sighed, deeply. "Happy Holidays, Mr Marx." I softly smiled as I turned my head towards the Professor's desk. There was a small lit evergreen in a glowing shade of LED lights. "Doing anything fun this season's giving?" I asked.

"Yes, Sabie... My wife." He began in response to my question. "Her brother and his girlfriend are coming over for dinner in two days then it's Las Vegas, Nevada for three days."

"Sounds like fun." I replied with a warm smile upon my face. "My cousin, Nina is getting married, come December." I walked towards the tables and chairs near the blackboard. I placed my bag onto the table. I pulled my tablet out from my bag along with my stylus. "I'm going to be a bridesmaid." I took the chair in front of me and I sat down.

"Tell your cousin, congratulations for me."

"Of course, Mr Marx."

# WANTS A WIN

As film class dove into thirty minutes, it was finally my turn to state my case about the film I picked out to break down. I walked towards the front of the class as everyone's judging eyes glared at me in silence. I took a deep breath before I spoke out what I had to say. It was a speech I've written over and over again.

Threw out the drafted letters as I recited the one that I polished. "To my fellow Seniors, we had a blast trying to out bitch each other throughout these four years." I read off the sheet of paper. "I'm not sure if you all wonder how much shit we will all take than High School." I chuckled while the other's whined. "I'm not sure if you all are seeing this in my point of view." I said as I lifted my eyes off the piece of paper. "It's the point of realising how lucky you are until all of your luck runs out. It's the fairytale, dreamers longed for. Not at all, the perfect girl. But I will be the fearless leader, the Alpha type."

My gaze dotted between Dylan Delano and Tanson Gutenberg. I sighed, softly. "It'll be easier...if I were a man." I paused for a few moments long. "Everyone would believe me. Everyone wouldn't think I'm looking for trouble. Or cause it." I folded the piece of paper in my hand. "I don't need to win."

I rolled my eyes as Tanson mocked me in plain sight. "It's Desdemona who said, beshrew me if I do such a wrong for the world." I saw Dylan do the same. The pair chuckled together even high five-ing. "If that's the case, I'd rather die a thousand times than see myself through their eyes." I lifted my shoulders into a shrug. "Now, I bid you adieu." I curtsied before returning to my seat.

"Tanson Gutenberg." Mr Marx called out. "You're up!"

Tanson got off of his seat and walked towards the front of the class. He turned around as he fixed his denim jacket. "That was... very deep, Jazzy." He began as he pulled out a sheet of paper in his pocket. He unfolded it. He read it. "Thank you for the four years I've spent joking around in the background and serenading girls in the hallway." He sighed, slightly crumpling the piece of paper in his hands. "You all probably think that I'm just the music man. I'm not!"

He's got everything.

Tanson's got everything.

I pity him, sometimes.

I quietly sighed.

"Don't get me wrong. I want to do music, but." Tanson paused, a while. "I grew up around music, especially Rhythm and Blues music."

# TOO OPTIMISTIC

I had no plans to follow my Auntie Ria's footsteps in pursuing a career on Broadway. She had the talents, the voice, the star quality. She was the gift. My Auntie Ria was and still is the pride of the family. There's nothing in this entire world that could top what she's done for the Gomez name.

I took a deep breath before I walked towards the school's auditorium through its stage door. It was the Senior Graduation meeting.

"Seniors!" The head of the graduation committee exclaimed. "We've decided on your student speaker." Her green eyes dotted around the auditorium. "And my God, this student's reputation for being the most important change, this school had ever seen." She picked up the stack of papers behind her and handed them out to the entire seventy-something seventeen-eighteen year old, sitting down. "Not only does this student have a famous Aunt." She continued as everyone muttered from behind me. "She deserves this!" She exclaimed with pride. "Jasmine Barnby."

I pointed to myself in shock as the head of the graduation committee nodded. Her red locks bobbing and bouncing along. I curled my lips into a smile. "Thank you." I mouthed.

The redhead smiled. "Next up is the student entertainment, which obviously goes to Tanson Gutenberg and his guitar."

"Yes!" Tanson celebrated. He gave the redhead a wink. "I will sing everyone a song that will leave an imprint on your kinds."

"Okay." She rolled her eyes and huffed as she looked over the sheets of paper in her hands. "Moving on to the next thing, the student short about your graduating class. Dylan Delano, are you up for the challenge?"

"Yes, ma'am." Dylan responded. "I'd be more than honoured to whip something up in time for graduation."

I pulled out my journal and a pen. "Can I have everyone's attention?" I spoke out.

"Please, take the stage, Jasmine." The redhead responded, gesturing for the graduating class to take a seat.

I stood up. I walked out of the row in which I sat. I carefully walked up the steps and towards the center of the stage. "Before we take our diplomas, make that final walk. My fellow graduates. I have a plan in which we go out with a bang. Of course, it does involve speaking in a manner of full fluency." I held my right hand up, a ninety degree angle and a decent amount of centimeters above my head. "I shall not quote the immortal words of the Queen B, but the great Bard, himself." I stated. "All those in favour of the Bard?"

A few hands rose up.

"How about of the famous Blonde, herself, Elle Woods?" I asked my fellow graduates.

Everyone, except for Dylan and Tanson, rose their hands.

"Then so be it." I concluded. "A quote from the famous Blonde, it will be."

# DOES NOTHING RIGHT

It's been months and months of preparation for this. I saw my cousin, smiling and happy. She finally found her perfect happy ending that she well-deserved after she drew her sword for her finally battle. I envied her so much. I couldn't bear to tell her how much I wanted for her to follow her heart and not her own mind.

"Jasmine, are you okay?" Mr Marx asked as I turned around, wiping the tears coming from the corner of my eyes. "What's wrong?"

I lightly nodded. "She got what she wanted." I said in response. "I don't get it. I'll never get it." I turned my head to face my cousin whose still engaged in a conversation in the distance. "It's wrong what had happened to them but I've learned so much from them. It was like something that consumed you as it takes its final victim." I sighed. "I don't know what made me a pretty good prey, or hunter."

My English Literature teacher placed a hand on my shoulder. "What do you mean?" He asked.

"I mean, she got her wish." I told Mr Marx.

I walked towards my fellow graduates, finding my place in line like the fourth grade. They all wanted to win the top award for graduating. I just wanted for this to be all over so that I didn't have to see them again but over seems like a light years away as their voice grew louder. I could barely hear myself think. I could barely breath.

I sighed as I pulled out my phone. I saw a notification pop up. It was from my cousin, Mary. "Okay." I said to myself.

Ate can't come in
but she sends her
congratulations.
—Mary

"Okay." I repeated.

# EASY TO LOVE

I walked up to the podium. I placed my scraps of paper on top of the podium's desk. I adjusted the microphone to my height, accordingly. I was shorter than the student before me. I sighed. "My fellow graduates, teachers, staff, and parents." I paused. "Throughout my four years of High School, the phrase 'it gets better' rolls off my tongue everyday, especially to those struggling with finding their own sense of identity."

I looked out to the audience and I noticed a sea of silence. It wasn't what I expected for a graduation. "I did too." I continued. "I kept to myself knowing that it'll only destroy my mentality. It's funny how I'm lifting everyone's spirits up but I wasn't doing myself anything good."

I lifted my head off my scraps of paper. "It seemed easy to do." I confessed. "Easy that I've hurt myself in the process. Sure that I've failed Spanish, but. I picked myself up. It got better. I did that."

I reached for the scraps of paper and I folded it. I stared at it for a few moments of the hands of time. It was a few moments for myself. "So, that next time someone asks if how the hell you've made it past High School without crying." I spoke as I turned my head to face my fellow graduates. "Tell them, 'what, like it's hard?'." I curled my lips into a smile before I returned to my seat.

It truly gets better.

# SANTA BABY

*A Short Story*

# ONE

Morning came, I grabbed pillow the beside me and I dragged it on top of my head. It was brighter than the summer sun outside from the overnight snowstorm. I hate how mornings kills my mood and vibe. I screamed into the pillow. I tossed the pillow onto the floor before I turned myself around to bury my face onto the pillow.

Stupid. Stupid. Stupid.

I punched the pillow repeatedly. "So stupid!" I said to myself. "I'm so stupid."

"What did the pillow ever do to you?" My pregnant sister, Ate Nina said, her voice bright like her smile as she stood there, rubbing her belly.

I turned around. I narrowed my eyes. "Easy for you to say." I retorted. "You're not the one who screwed it up with her boyfriend. Thomas loves you. Max doesn't even want to talk to me and it's awkward enough that he's around during the baby shower yesterday and won't even talk to me."

She lifted her shoulders into a shrug. I couldn't tell if she's going to argue with me or agree with me. My Ate Nina isn't always the precise person when it comes to giving people advice. She just says it how it is. "I don't know, Mary, but there's a film crew for you downstairs." She sat on the bottom of my bed. "It's for that TV show you like. What's it called again?"

"Who Do You Think You Are?" I said as I sat up. I reached for her belly to feel the baby's kick. "I finally get to find out what happened between Lola Elise and Lolo Franklin in the 1920s."

"And Mamma Emilda during the Spanish Colonisation." She added. "I wonder what she did."

"Probably, she hustled her way into a Spaniard's pants." I joked.

She moved my hand to the other side of her belly. "Or an American, she lived during the 1800s, after all." She pointed out.

"True."

We both giggled.

"Boy or girl?" I asked her as I felt the baby's kick through her belly. "Have you two picked out a name yet?"

"No, not yet." She responded as she carefully stood up off the bed. "But if it's a girl, I'm hoping to name her, Hope Cynthia. If it's a boy, Milagro Christoph."

I got myself out of bed. I picked up my iPhone off the bedside table. "What about him?" I said as I picked up my zipped-up sweater off the floor and I put it on. "What does he want to name the baby?"

"Thomas jr." She responded without a single hesitation to her voice. "I told him that he's dreaming and he retorts by asking me what kind of name is Milagro."

# TWO

I walked down the stairs. I saw my sister in the kitchen on the phone. She looked like she was crying and mad.

"I hate you." She cried. She was triggered by the conversation between her and Thomas, who was on the other side of the phone call. "You're supposed to be here with me." She dropped down onto the floor, crying.

Our mother pulled her off the ground and she gave her a hug. "It'll be okay." She assured her as she held my sister close in her arms. "It'll be okay, Anak."

I walked into the living room and I saw a group of people each holding a mug in their hands. "Hey, Happy Snow Day." I said. "Just tell me what I have to do." I walked towards the film crew. "Excuse me!"

A tall, dark haired male walked towards me with a grin on his face. He seemed like one of those boys who just walked out of an Usher music video. "You must be Mary Gomez." He said as he put a hand out for me to shake. "I'm Stuart Jones. It's a pleasure to meet you. I'm a fan of your show."

I eyed his hand before I analysed his posture. "Likewise." I responded as I folded my arms over my chest. I rolled my eyes.

"Uhh..." He scratched the top of his head. "So, we do need you to sit on the floor on a laptop face-timing people or just looking up your family history with your mom and sister."

"That's great." I retorted. I wasn't in the mood for a conversation. "Thanks."

# THREE

I walked down the sidewalk. I felt the crunch of the snow as my boots pressed against the ground. No one was driving on the road and every car covered with inches and inches of snow. I slipped my hands into my coat's pocket and looked at the kids playing on the hill. "Be careful." I told them.

Such a déjà vu...
High School!

I softly chuckled as I squatted down and pulled out my hands from my coat's pockets. I reached for the snow and started to gather some snow together. I stood up and patted the snow into a ball before I threw it towards the kids. "Come and get me!" I called out as the kids started to prepare their ice cold weapon.

"It's on, Auntie Mary!" One of my old friends's kids exclaimed. The kid had an off-the-shoulder length black hair and side bangs. She also had on a white snow coat that I used to wear when I was fifteen years old. She placed her fist towards her shoulder then threw the snowball towards me.

I turned myself around and dodged the snowball coming towards me. I gasped as I accidentally bumped into a stranger. "Oh my gosh, I'm so sorry, love." I said as I placed my hands back inside of my coat's pockets. "Are you okay?"

"I'm fine."

I furrowed my brows and sighed. "What are you doing here?" I questioned. I was furious, mad, angry. All wrapped up into one boiling pot of hot lava. "You and your black ass just managed to find their way to Oregon. Get over yourself, Max! You had your chance."

He shrugged. "Baby girl, I'm not here for us." He responded, his voice at an irritating manner to my eardrums, as I rolled my eyes. "I'm here for your sister." He pulled out a folded up envelope out of his pocket. "And apparently, her and Tom likes to keep it old school and not use email like a normal human being of this century."

I took the envelope from his hand and began opening it.

"What are you doing?" He said, trying to grab the envelope from my hands.

"No." I replied as I pulled out a folded up piece of paper out of the envelope. I unfolded the piece of paper and began reading it.

Dearest Nina,
I am waiting for you, just counting down the days to see you again. I couldn't phone you or anything since Vancouver is infested with a snowstorm and it's to risky for me to drive down there to see you.

"That's not for you." He protested as he attempted to take the piece of paper from my hands for the second time.

Tsk. Tsk. I curled my lips into a mischievous smile. "I thought that you knew me by now." I told him before I continued on reading.

Benedict and Sophie gives their hello and their sincere congratulations.

"Come on, Mary."

"Not yet!" I argued before I pushed on.

Max is sulking. I don't know what to tell him. He seems like he misses your sister so much. Can you tell your sister that he is sorry? I'm afraid if she doesn't see that he's changed then I don't know what will.

He loves her.

He told me himself.

"You...love me!?" I said as I folded the piece of paper back up, slipped it back into the envelope, and handed it to him. "Y'know, when Tom writes a letter, I thought it'll be just on how much he misses her but no, Max. This is different, this is way, way different."

"I don't want to deal with this right now, Mary." He started to walk away.

"Tell me THE truth!" I yelled as I followed him, placing my hand on his arm and turned him around to face me. "Do you love me or not?"

"I said I don't want to deal with this right now." He said, his voice raising in volume. "Just leave it, Mary. You don't want a fight out here in the open, I know you." He folded the envelope and slipped it into his pocket.

"Try me." I told him.

He placed his hands on my cheeks and kissed me.

I pulled back from the kiss before I slapped him across the face.

# FOUR

I pulled the duvet cover close to my body as I turned to face him. I placed my hand on his chest. I looked up at him and chuckled. "Are we going to keep on doing this?"

"Doing what?" He asked, curiously.

"This?" I said as I sat up with my hand on the bed. "Cat and mouse and watch dogs bark at each other, every now and then." I laid back down on the bed as I picked up the remote control from the bedside table and turned the TV on.

"I get it, baby girl." He took the remote control from my hand and switched the channel to E! News. He chuckled as he gestured his hand towards the TV. "How can your sister not see this shit?" He turned his head towards me. "Tom is out partying with a few models while she's at home waiting to pop."

I kept my eyes glued to the TV screen. "Yeah." I said, shaking my finger towards the TV. "I can't believe that they are letting famous males get away with this shit." I picked up my iPhone off the bedside table and unlocked it.

He took my iPhone off my hands and placed it on top of the beside table. "Don't you dare tell your sister." He told me. "For their baby's sake."

"He is going to break her heart." I protested.

"How can you say that?" He argued. "He has to find time to talk to her on the phone."

"She's been sitting around and wait for him get back home." I leaned over to pick up my clothes off the floor before I walked into the bathroom. "It's so hard to see her pretending like nothing is wrong and hearing her cry in her own fucking room." I slipped on my panty on and hooked my bra on.

"What?!" I heard him say.

I slipped on my jeans and put my sweater shirt on. "Yeah." I said as I walked out of the bathroom. "That's all that she does, Mabie." I walked towards the bed and sat down. "But I'm sure that they'll find a way to figure things out once he's done filming. Maybe hit the sack? Or go nursery shopping?"

"Those sounds like great options for them."

I picked up my shoes and started to put them on, beginning with the left. "Well, you don't know my sister like I do."

"You're right." He said as he picked up his clothes off the floor and started to put them on. "That's why I'm not going to discuss this." He sat down as he buttoned his shirt up. "They're life is not our life to discuss."

"I guess, you're right."

# FIVE

I walked into the living room and placed my house keys on top of the coffee table. I looked out the window. It started snowing again. I huffed in disbelief, rolling my eyes in the process. "Thank you, Canada." I said, sarcastically. I turned around and walked towards the kitchen. "Hey…"

"Hey…" She smiled, weakly. "Where did you go off to?"

"Max." I responded. "With Max." I placed a brown teddy bear on top of the kitchen counter and sat down on the stool next to her. "Anything happened with Tom, yesterday?"

She slid her iPhone towards me as she remained silent staring at the teddy bear on top of the kitchen counter. This was unlike her.

I pulled picked up her iPhone.

Actor, Thomas Clifford has been 'married to pregnant girlfriend, Nina Gomez for months and we didn't notice'

The article was written by Joan Elliott.

Clifford, 37 at the time, now 38 and Gomez, 23 spent three nights in Las Vegas together days after Thanksgiving. The couple was seen leaving a a chapel near the Strip sources says that the two had gotten eloped in the chapel by themselves.

Pictures recently surfaced of Gomez looking very pregnant which was confirmed by Gomez herself during her interview with Olympia Griffiths on February 6th.

At the same time, Clifford celebrated his 38th birthday in Vancouver, British Columbia and Gomez was nowhere in sight. We immediately thought that the couple went their separate ways after New Year's Day.

"I'm very happy to have met [Nina]. She's unlike what people make of her." Clifford told Vanity Fair. "She's complex and a boss. I've never met anyone so in control of their own career like she is."

I sighed as she picked up the teddy bear off the kitchen counter and placed it on her lap.

"I admire [Thomas]. He is an incredibly talented person and he loves what he does." Gomez told Hollywood Reporter.

The two seems like good friends with no bad blood between them.

We reached to the pair's teams to clarify and we didn't get any responses back.

Only time will tell, where the couple is at.

"You've got hitched in Vegas and you didn't tell me?!" I was shocked.

# THE OLD NOEL

*A Short Story*

# THEODORE'S SURVIVING JOURNAL PAGES

1 October 1762

*This is torture. This is terrible torture. I'm 32 and I'm stuck in another country fighting off the Spanish. God help me survive this. I need to survive this.*

6 October 1762

*It's all over. I can rest easy if that's even a possibility.*

16 November 1762

*While I was taking a stroll on the grounds of Manilla, I saw a woman with a basket on her head. She seemed startled when I approach her. She was beautiful and exotic looking. I began to wonder if she spoke a word of English. One can dream. She put the backet down and picked up a stick off the ground. "Hoy!" she exclaimed. My mind spoke too soon. "I'm sorry to have intruded on your land, sweetheart." I told her. "I'm a little lost. Would you mind helping me?"*

27 December 1762

*I spent the whole entire Christmas with her because I wanted to. She's hospitable, crazy, sweet, and an angel. Her name is Josefina Ayala.*

14 January 1763

*I'm teaching Josephine some English before I laid with her. She's an excellent student and a quick learner.*

21 February 1763

He drew her.

6 April 1763

*I can't believe that William Draper and Samuel Cornish just moved George Beaufort, Newton Rutledge, and James Wielemaker into the same part of Manilla as I am. I'm not at all pleased but Captain's orders, I guess. I just hope that the darling Josephina is okay with the whole thing going on in her village.*

17 June 1763

*I'm a monster. I didn't want to do it but she was helpless. I had to protect her. I hadn't have any choice.*

30 December 1763

*If she wasn't a native of Manilla, maybe people I know would love her for who she is and not for her exotic looks and personality.*

## 24 March 1764

*I don't want to leave her. I can't leave her alone. She's everything to me.*

## 16 May 1764

*It pains me to have to tell her goodbye when I've already fallen in love with her. I just hope that she will be okay wherever life takes the angel.*

# PRESENT DAY

## *Christmas Eve*

I opened the drawer in Thomas's new office. I picked up a cream-coloured manila folder labeled 'Emilda J. Ayala' and placed it on top of the desk. I closed the drawer as I opened the folder. I took a deep breath and sighed. I picked up an photo copy of sketch of a woman with long raven hair. It was the only surviving photograph of my great-great-great-great grandmother, Mamma Emilda.

"What are you doing in here?" A familiar voice said as I turned my head towards the doorway. "Darling, we have guest out there." He closed the door behind him. He walked towards me and gave me a kiss on the cheek.

"I know." I responded as I handed him the sketch. "I finally found her, Tom. I thought for months that Mary was kidding about me being like her but I understand it now."

He looked at the sketch of my Mamma Emilda in his hands. "I'm not surprised." He said, placing the sketch down on top of the desk. "She's beautiful."

"That's what he said."

"Hey!" He exclaimed, softly chuckling.

I handed him a photocopy of a journal entry dated December twenty second seventeen sixty-two. An author wasn't mentioned on the photocopy. "Just read it." I told him.

And he did.
The piece of paper reads:

> *I am so sure of Theodore's love for this woman is just to feel her bosom in a warm embrace. I do not understand how she is all that until I saw her. She looked like a piece of heaven that the Lord sent to rescue us all. She is just a beauty of the exotic kind. I need to take her away from Theodore but how? That is the question.*

I stood up and pulled the chair out before I leaned against the desk.

He sat down on the chair, placing the photocopy down on top of the desk. He pulled me towards him.

I turned around and sat down on his lap of t. I turned my head and kissed him on the lips as he wrapped his arms around my waist. I placed my hand on top of his chest as I pulled back from the kiss. "It's still early." I said as I laid my head on his shoulder. "I love you."

He placed a hand on my belly.

I lifted my head off his shoulder. I reached for another photocopy out of the folder and handed it to him. I rested my head on top of his shoulder again as he held the photocopy in his hand.

The document was written by Jane Hallewell, a widow of Theodore Marriott's who survived him by thirteen years.

It reads:

> *Theodore left so many fortunes to his children and the manor to me and our eldest son. William Clifford who was fifteen at the time of his death. I never wanted to be the woman who is second best to a woman who he had met and been with for twenty months while he was in Manila. I do not wish her ill as I have not seen her for myself and I do not know if I could ever see her for myself. She is the last word he spoke.*

# THE LETTERS FROM GEORGE BEAUFORT TO JOSEFINA AYALA AND THEODORE C. MARRIOTT

17 March 1764

*Dearest Josefina,*

*As you maybe know that Theodore has to leave his post in your village and I was sent to watch over an rebels against British occupy. I've been told of your hospitlity by Theodore himself. I do want to continue his teachings of the English language to you and your village. If you'd like.*

*George Beaufort*

25 March 1764

*Theodore C. Marriott,*

*You should be the one watching over this village and not me. I'm quite the worse person for this job. The lass you've spoke about his heaven sent. I spoke to her about continueing her studies in the English language.and in reading and writing. I'd like to have you visit Josefina when you have the time. It is the least that I could do.*


*George Beaufort*

# PRESENT DAY

## *Christmas Eve, Midnight*

I placed a hand on his back and gave him a hug. "Merry Christmas, Babe." I whispered in his ear before I handed him my glass of sparkling water. I pealed myself from the side hug.

"Where are you going?" He asked in a whispered tone as he held my hand.

"The bathroom." I told him before I walked out of the room. I walked towards the steps and sat down, holding on the railings and pressed my forehead against the back of my hand. I took a deep breath and sighed. I placed my other hand on my belly and rubbed lightly it.

I stood up and pulled myself off the steps. I placed my hand under my belly as I pulled myself up the steps. I placed a hand on the wall and walked towards my room. I sat down on top of my bed and laid my head down.

I screamed as I panted. I heard the clinging of glasses placed down on top of the table and the footsteps running up the steps and into my room. I turned my head and saw Thomas and Mrs Roberts walk into my room. I took a gasp of air.

Thomas walked towards me and held my hand. "Darling..." He said as Mrs Roberts grabbed a bowl from under my bed.

"Keep her occupied while I put some lukewarm water into this bowl." She told him before she walked into my bathroom.

I pulled his hand and placed it on top of my forehead as I panted, grasping for air. I turned my head towards him and burst into tears. I felt the sheets under me get wetter and wetter. "I think I'm going into labour." I told him in between sobs. I took a deep breath and panted. I squeezed his hand tightly. "Tom..."

"Darling, want me to call a Doctor?" He asked. With his right hand, he reached for his pocket and pulled out his iPhone.

I shook my head. "Just tell me about Theodore and Jane." I responded, blowing a several puffs of air out of my mouth.

"Alright, darling." He said, putting his iPhone back inside of his pocket. "What would you like to know?"

"Did he love her?" I asked as Mrs Roberts walked back into the room.

She placed the bowl on top of the bedside table.

"Not likely." He replied, placing a hand on my left cheek. "He was and might've been still in love with Josefina for all that I know. My great-great-great-great grandmother Jane Hallewell couldn't compete with the lost of Josefina. The news of Josefina's death left a whole in his heart."

She walked towards the chest located at the foot of my bed and opened it. She lifted the top up and pulled out a small box with her left hand. She closed the chest and walked towards the bedside table. She placed the box on top.

# THE LETTERS FROM THEODORE C. MARRIOTT TO JANE HALLEWELL, A FORMER ENGLISH DEBUTANTE

28 June 1764

He sent her a drawing of her.

18 September 1765

*My darling, Jane,*

*You are sunlight to my darkness. You are an angel from heaven. You are not what I've longed for but you are what I needed in my life. I love you so much my darling.*

*Yours,*

*Theodore Marriott*

6 December 1766

*My darling, Jane,*

*I have inherited my father's Manor and all of it's servants. I'm not sure if I could do anything about it but my life is goof for now. I want you to come to Haywood Florentine Manor and be my wife as I can not find a day in my life without you.*

*Yours,*

*Thedore Marriott*

16 February 1767

*My darling, Jane,*

*I wish nothing more than anything than to be with you my love. I've had so many people ask me about you in court. My dear, you should have been here with me. King George the Third requested for the whole troop and their wives in court for a grand ball of sort. I have sent for a carriage for you and your young sister, Ethlinda to pick you up at Haywood Florentine Manor. I love you, darling.*

*Yours,*

*Theodore Marriott*

13 April 1767

*My darling, Jane,*

*I'm going home very soon, my darlin,g but I am not all by myself. My fellow soldiers will come along for the ride. I have not any chance to talk to you during the grand ball as I was taken by surprise by some gossip thast arose that night. It was absurd and nothing to worry about, my dear. It was all baffoonary during my time in Manilla with a local girl who I've taught English to. She's nothing more than a mere student of mine.*

*Yours,*

*Thedore Marriott*

18 August 1768

*My darling, Jane,*

*I'm truly sorry for leaving all so sudden. I just heard some dreadful news about a student of mine. I had to see it for myself, my love. The news broke my heart but I was greeted by a Spanish Lady, Emilda Gomez-Collado and a Spanish Lord, Teodoro Gomez-Collado. They're such a sight to see. A couple worth learning from, my dear. I love for you to see them before they leave for Spain. I will see to it that you are sent for to meet them.*


*Yours,*


*Theodore Marriott*

# SEPTEMBER OF 1768

I lightly bowed my head, walking towards the small tea table. "Miss Gomez-Collado." I said. "It's a pleasure to meet you since you're arrival here in London."

She lightly bowed her head in return. "Forgive me, Señor Marriott." She spoke, her Spanish accent blossomed as she gestured to the seat next to her. "I do not know much of your English." She curled her lips into a smile before she took a sip of her tea. She placed the tea cup down on top of the saucer. "Um... Encantado de conocerte, Señor Marriott."

"That's alright, Miss Gomez-Collado." I reassured her. I placed my hand on top of hers. "But do forgive me and my nosey ways, may I ask why a Spaniard like you is here in London?"

"My daughter, Estrella Teodoria María Alvarez Gomez-Collado." She responded, picking up a macaroon off of the plate in front of her and took a small bite. She placed a hand in front of her mouth as she placed the macaroon back down on top of the plate. "She is about cuatro años de edad. Su padre, mi esposo, quería que ella estudiara inglés y latín aquí en Londres. Lo siento, Señor Marriott." She stood up off her seat and walked towards the door.

I turned around and watched. My arm resting on top of the seat's back rest.

Her eyes glued to a piece of paper in her hands as she gestured for the maid to leave the room. She walked towards the tea table, reading in silence. She took a deep breath and sighed. "El escándalo me sigue a todas partes." She muttered as she placed a hand on her forehead and shook her head.

I reached for her hand and took it off of her forehead. "What's the matter, Miss Gomez-Collado?" I asked her in a polite manner.

"Mi esposo fue visto con otra mujer y para un Católico que es algo que no será tolerado de manera amable." She said in rage as she snatched her hand away from my grasp before she walked towards the fireplace and tossed the piece of paper into the fire. "Esto no será un problema mientras las noticias permanezcan en esta sala y en ningún otro lugar. Señor Marriott... ¿Por favor?"

"Forgive my false Spanish, Miss Gomez-Collado." I told her. "Eres un placer estar cerca. Él volverá a sus sentidos. ¡Marca mi palabra!" My Spanish prononciation was off putting to my own ears and possibly hers too.

She softly chuckled.

"What is it?" I asked her.

"Your false Spanish is funny, Señor."

I chuckled. "Worth the try, Miss Gomez-Collado." I spoke as I picked up a macaroon off of her plate and took a bite of it.

Her brown eyes sparkled as a ray of sunlight hit it. Her face was lit up with a warm and welcoming smile. "Señor Marriott, you are a soldier, yes?" She said, her voice was eager and full of optimism. "You have seen many beautiful places, yes?"

I lightly nodded my head. "Manila was my latest venture outside of London." I replied, picking up a napkin off of the tea table. "A girl I once knew passed away. She would've been twenty-three years of age now."

"Lo siento, Señor." She said, reaching for my hand. "It is a difficult time for you, no?"

I lightly nodded my head in response as I took a deep breath and sighed. "Forgive my current state, Miss Gomez-Collado." I told her as I picked up my leather bound journal off the tea table. "I am in no state to take up the time of a lady of your status." I stood up and lightly bowed my head. I walked towards the door. I reached for the doorknob as I heard the sliding of a chair and footsteps coming towards me. I felt a hand on my arm. I turned my head and saw her standing beside behind me.

She had a tear running down her face. "Will you stay with me, Señor?"

"I will." I turned around and tossed my journal onto the floor before I picked her up off the ground and walked towards the bed. I laid her down on top of the bed and I brushed a hair strand away from her face.

She reached for my cheek.

I grabbed her hand and brought it towards my chest before I leaned in and kissed her on the lips. I couldn't stop myself. It was a curse that was bestowed upon my manhood after I've spoken to a woman with a bewitching personality.

# FINALE

I've loved writing ever since I was a little girl but if I stopped dreaming I wouldn't be the girl that I am today. I've been called delusional because I love what I love. And I just love people so much even though I'm drastically the shyest girl you'll ever meet. I always have to do something with my hands or I'll get bored.

The funny thing about my boredom is that I'm the only one who knows how to cure it. And shopping is out of the question. Wanderlust is.

I've been to so many places. Spain. Greece. France. Sweden. British Columbia. My passport has been stamped for my ventures around the world. I've been jet lagged a few times but never cried when I left the Philippines. I wanted so much but to see the world is something that my heart can take. And that's not me being poetic!

I just love the idea of seeing something new. Boy, it's a little crazy to see the breathtaking view that is Barcelona, Spain. Or walk with the natives of Santorini, Greece. Or visit family in Stockholm, Sweden. Or turning eighteen in Victoria, British Columbia in Canada. Or even walk with princesses in Disneyland Paris in France. I did and saw all that. I want to see more.

Live in your daydreams,
Maria
xo

PS. Always remember. That your culture does not define you who truly are.

# TRANSLATIONS

Encantado de conocerte, Señor
I'm pleased to meet you, Mister

Cuatro años de edad
Four years of age

Su padre, mi esposo, quería que ella estudiara inglés y latín aquí en Londres
Her father, my husband wanted for her to study English and Latin here in London

Lo siento, Señor
I'm sorry, Mister

El escándalo me sigue a todas partes
The scandal follows me everywhere

Mi esposo fue visto con otra mujer y para un católico que es algo que no será tolerado de manera amable
My husband was seen with another woman and for a Catholic that is something that will not be tolerated in a kind way

Esto no será un problema mientras las noticias permanezcan en esta sala y en ningún otro lado
This will not be a problem as long as the news remains in this

room and nowhere else

¿Por favor?
Please?

Eres un placer estar cerca. Él volverá a sus sentidos. ¡Marca mi palabra!
You are a pleasure to be close. He will return to his senses. Mark my word!

# MEMO

To the folks over at Kindle Direct Publishing, thank you for all of the helpful tips and tricks that you guys have told me. I wouldn't have figured out what was wrong with my manuscript without those tips. To Sabina Fenn, for the illustration of the girl blowing the bubble. To Ben Dawley, for the front and back cover. To Shelly Corbett, for the Lego Loki photograph that I so much love and admire. To the folks over at Portland Community College, thanks for all of the life lessons that I've learned along the way. You all made me into the woman that I am today. To Conte Bennett. To Mr Kevin Bennett, thanks for allowing me to blossom into the film guru that I am today. To David Sikking, thanks for letting me shine in your class. To Barbara Peterson and Beth Fitzgerald, thanks for everything.

To the inspirational woman that is Taylor Swift, your music has been the soul inspiration for writing each small little detail in each poem that's quite personal to me. Even though, I can not share every single little detail of my personal life into my poetry just yet. I'm holding back on that for now. To Doreen aka Kate Kingsbury, thanks for being another one of my greatest inspirations. To Abigail Adams, Corazon Aquino, Joan of Arc, Gabriela Silang, Queen Cleopatra and the other women who came before me. All the lessons that you all taught me will be kept inside of my heart. I idolise each and everyone of you. To Sarah and Angelique, you two are my closest friends like ever!!! I love you both!!

To my mother, thanks for everything. I love you loads. To my #sistahhs, Janna, Francine, & Danielle, may the rest of our lives be the best of our lives. To my brother, Gavin Ernest Mendoza, you're so special and I will always remind you that you are actually smarter than I am. To my step-dad, Gil Mendoza, thanks for being the father that I never had in life. My Aunts, Uncle, Cousins. My grandparents, especially Lakambini Constantino and Maria Batara. I love you guys so much. Angelique. Sarah. I love you girls so much!!!

To Tom, thanks for playing one of cinema's greatest characters. To Hardy, thanks for being one of my the Toms that I'm inspired by. To Holland, remember when I chickened out on doing flips at Trafalgar Square? No? Me either;) Jeff Goldblum, thanks for the pet talk about age gap in relationships and for telling me that everyone makes mistakes. It's a lesson that I will never forget. I love you for that. Shawn, thanks for putting up with my crazy way back when. Taylor and Joe; My favourite couple of all time. I get so happy whenever I see photographs of you two together.

To the people who judged me so much to hurt me... I guess, you're the soul topic of my poems about heartbreak. I don't hate you I just wouldn't be writing about you if you weren't so cruel and called me a rebel. You know who you are.

To the Avakin Life Community, I love you guys so much. I wouldn't have decided to publish a book without you guys. To C Jin Lovelace (aka ATOH Project). To Product and her fantastic films. To my ASF family. To the Lockwood family in England. There's so many of you to name who inspired me so much. This blonde loves each and everyone of you. I also hate that I had to leave all of a sudden but I will always treasure the memories we've made.

To the staff at Unity (Legacy Health), thanks for everything! I know that I just journal too much and completed 6-ish notebooks while I was there. To Kyle, you can do it boo!!!!!! To Leah Dooley, it's great to meet another Asian-American writer. I hope to buy your work soon. To all of the patients still there in Unity, soon you'll get better.

To my lovely readers, I wouldn't be here without each and everyone of you. Your kindness means so much to me. I love you guys so much!!!! And I promise that I read everything that you guys write to me, I'm just super busy with life that I can not respond to each and every single one of you. And I read your fanfictions too;) You are all so creative in what you all do. That's why I love crazy!!!!!

# ABOUT THE AUTHOR

## Maria Eloise Baza

Maria Baza was born to a middle class family as Laika Mari Constantino Batara in Mandaluyong City, Philippines. She was raised in Abergavenny, Wales, United Kingdom by the time that she turned 7 years old. She had a few run-ins with her Catholic background so by the time that she immigrated to the United States. She did not enjoy her days growing up in Beaverton, Oregon. Baza was enrolled into Art School in 2010 and graduated along with the Class of 2014 with passing grades.

She loves Musical Theater and the Motion Pictures. She also loves Disney films and listening to music in her spare time. Her favorite singers are Taylor Swift, Bruno Mars, Selena Gomez, Lady Gaga, Kesha, Nicki Minaj just to name a few.

At the tender age of 24, she began to write her own poetry and posted them on her Wordpress blog. She voluntarily checked into a rehabilitation clinic called Unity in February 2020 and is now out of rehab and prepared to start over with a whole new beginning with a new and improved blog and website.

Follow Maria on Twitter and Instagram
@MsMariaBaza

Made in the USA
Coppell, TX
02 September 2020